W9-DCW-828

Contents:

For my friend Jens Kargaard,
a modern–day Livingstone in the primitive
bush country of South Africa.

David Livingstone

The Missionary
Who "Discovered" Africa

1813 —1873

Great men and women are not in need of our praise.
We are the ones in need of getting to know them.

By Ben Alex

Illustrations by Giuseppe Rava

VICTOR BOOKS

A DIVISION OF SCRIPTURE PRESS PUBLICATIONS INC.
USA CANADA ENGLAND

INTO AFRICA

We're going on a trip. It'll be a long, hard trip, probably the toughest trip you'll ever make. So pack your things—and don't forget your hiking boots, insect repellant and sunblock. We're going to Africa.

To get to the place where our trip begins we'll take an airplane across the Sahara desert down to the equator. From there we'll turn south, drop over the mountains, across **Lake Edward** and continue until we hit a blue lake stretching south as far as the eye can see: **Lake Tanganyika**.

Look over to your left! On the distant eastern shore you'll see the town of **Ujiji**; and further away, the deep jungles of Burundi and Tanzania.

To the West is the country of Zaire. As we descend, you'll see zebra and antelope, a lonely herd of giraffes or elephants. Our plane sweeps over a grove of bent trees, then hits the ground with a bump, rolls down the narrow runway and comes to a halt. As we step out we are met by a breeze that feels as hot as air from a giant hairdryer.

MEET DR. LIVINGSTONE

It's a bright, sultry summer afternoon. From the east, a dozen men wind their way slowly through the yellow grass. The Africans wear nothing but loincloths. They carry heavy packs on their heads. The sun glistens off their

sweaty backs. A tall white man limps in front of them. His face is lined with wrinkles, his brown hair streaked with grey. His beard and moustache are nearly white.

Though he seems exhausted and in pain, the man motions impatiently at his carriers that they should move faster. Finally, he points with his walking stick towards the soft grass under a tall **mvula** tree. There the group unloads its burdens and drops down into the grass.

The white man pulls out a metal-backed notebook, along with ink and pen from his travel bag, then sits down and sighs. "So many difficulties have been put in my way," he writes, "I'm doubting whether God is with me . . . ." He drops the notebook onto his lap and opens a well-worn Bible: "All power is given unto me in heaven and on earth: go ye, therefore, and teach all nations . . . and lo, I am with you always, even unto the end of the world."

This man is the Scottish missionary, doctor and explorer, **David Livingstone**. He is heading toward the end of his African adventure. Let's retrace his footsteps—and peek inside his journals. Along the way we will discover why David Livingstone is called the greatest explorer of the nineteenth century.

5

THE MASSACRE AT NYANGWE, 1871

On the following morning David Livingstone's African caravan reached the banks of the Lualaba river and market town of Nyangwe. Women in colorful clothes arranged their baskets of fish and displayed trays of sweet potatoes and corn. It was market day, and Dr. Livingstone's crew were stocking provisions before continuing their treck north along the river.

Africa Before Livingstone

When Livingstone arrived in South Africa in 1841, the map of the "dark African continent" was unlike our maps today except for the coastline. Portuguese explorers had accurately drawn that 350 years earlier: Bartolomeu Dias sailed along the western coast, reaching the Cape of Good Hope (1488). Ten years later, Vasco da Gama rounded the Cape and explored the eastern coastline, surprised to find wealthy Arab trading posts there. (These later became slave stations. By Livingstone's birth, an estimated 100,000 African slaves were being exported yearly to Arab countries, America and Brazil.)

Yet although the coastal regions and the lower streams of Africa's four great rivers—the Nile, the Niger, the Congo, and the Zambesi—had been mapped by Europeans,

This map shows Central Africa as it was known in 1841 when Livingstone arrived.

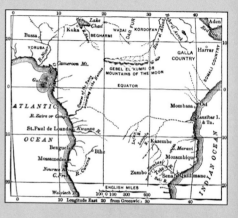

All the hustle and bustle made Livingstone cheerful, even though he was suffering from several tropical diseases. Four years earlier he had set out to solve an ancient mystery: Where did the great **Nile**, the world's longest river, begin? Explorers had wondered about the source of the Nile for thousands of years, yet no one had found it. The interior part of Africa had never been explored; no highways or railroads crossed the thick, impassable jungle. The only way through it was by riverboat.

If Livingstone could find the Nile's source and trace the river up to **Lake Victoria** in the north, then the interior of this dark continent would become open to European trade and colonization—and most importantly, to missionaries. Then the good news of the Gospel could be brought to the millions of African people who had never even heard of Jesus!

Nyangwe was the last place Livingstone could buy food before the difficult journey northwards along the Lualaba river. Livingstone felt optimistic as he bargained with the women at the market. He was convinced the Lualaba river would lead him to the Nile. In a few weeks he would be able to put the upper Nile on the map!

Then something happened which drastically changed his plans.

An African suddenly ran out of the forest into town, pointing at clouds of black smoke behind the trees.

"Slave traders!" he shouted. "Fire in our villages!"

Livingstone spun around just in time to see a gang of Arab men in white robes storming through the marketplace. The Arabs stopped and shot into the crowd. Children screamed and ran. Baskets and buckets were knocked

beyond them were enormous spaces marked "Unexplored" on maps of the 1800s. It was believed that the interior of Africa was one vast desert landscape. No European had ever been further north of the South African colony than the edge of the great Kalahari desert, where Dutch settlers, called Boers, moved after the English took over their colony and abolished slave labor on their farms.

Dr. David Livingstone, in 1849, was the first European to cross that desert and plunge into unexplored Central Africa.

"Africa is like a chest," he said. "The top and bottom

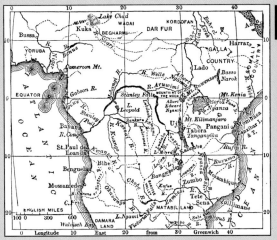

Central Africa as known shortly after Livingstone's death.

drawers have been pulled open. But the center drawer is locked tight."

over. Vegetables and fruit rolled onto the ground or splattered as they fell. Some Africans ran for the river and jumped into overloaded canoes; many were shot in the back by Arabs as others paddled madly with hands and arms to get away. The canoes turned over, and many people were swept away by the current. Their heads disappeared one by one under the water. Those left unharmed were hunted down and captured by the Arabs, then marched off to a slave station in Ujiji.

Livingstone was in shock. Around him lay wounded children, and from the river the cries of drowning people echoed through the village. More than three hundred were dead.

Later that day, Livingstone counted the clouds of smoke from different villages on fire around Nyangwe: seventeen. "Like being in Hell," he wrote in his journal. "I'm sick at heart! This place is a den of the worst kind of hunters!"

Never before—not even in times of tribal warfare—had women and children been attacked like this on their way to market. The slave traders were plunderers and murderers.

LOST IN THE JUNGLE

That night Livingstone was restless and could not sleep. He called **Susi**, his African servant.

"Tomorrow," he said, "we'll start out north along the Lualaba. It'll be a long and hard journey. Susi, what do you think our chances are?"

"Not good, **Bwana**," answered Susi. "Many carriers have deserted us. Bwana is sick. We have no medicine since the carrier bearing the medicine chest ran away in the forest. Chances not good, Bwana."

"What disturbs me," nodded Livingstone, "is that I cannot trust the Arabs anymore. In the past, the slave traders were kind to me. They helped us against hostile tribes on the trail. But after what happened at the market today, I will not accept another favor from them! I'm wondering if we should turn around and go back to Ujiji."

"How far to Ujiji?" asked Susi.

"Five hundred miles," replied Livingstone. "In Ujiji we can hire new carriers and pick up medicine. By the time we get there I'm sure the supplies I ordered up from the coast will have arrived."

Early next morning, Livingstone and his little caravan walked back along the same trail they had just travelled. Susi was watching the doctor's face, marred by pain with every step he took.

"Please rest!" said Susi as he gently helped Livingstone to lean against a tree before he took off his master's shoes and cleaned the huge sores on his feet.

The journey back to Ujiji took more than three months. All the while Livingstone became weaker, suffering from pneumonia with its fever, while his feet were covered with terrible sores. Finally, the caravan reached its destination—only to find that the medicine and supplies had been stolen!

Now all Livingstone could do was wait.

Tropical Diseases

Because Livingstone was a physician he was able to cure many deadly diseases among the Africans and thus earning their respect and protection. He was also able to cure himself from tropical illnesses. During his 32 years in Africa he suffered from malaria (fatal disease with violent fever caused by parasites in mosquitoes), dysentery (exhausting bowel disease that causes the body to lose too much fluid), ulcers (painful sores on his feet that "often lame permanently if they do not kill") and pneumonia (infectious lung disease).

The drugs that helped Livingstone survive were Quinine and Calomel. The photo shows some of the medicines and tools that Stanley took to him in 1872. Susi and Chuma, Livingstone's faithful servants, brought them back to England after Livingstone's death.

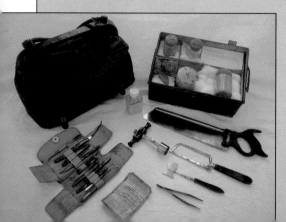

Some of Dr. Livingstone's medical tools

"DR. LIVINGSTONE, I PRESUME?"

But a miracle was on its way: A long, winding caravan was at that very moment heading toward Ujiji with 192 African carriers and more than six tons of supplies: medicine, food, kettles, cloth, blankets, tents—even a bathtub! One carrier bore the American flag. Beside him tramped a tall white man, leading the others. This was **Henry Morton Stanley**, a young reporter for the **New York Herald**, the world's largest sensationalistic newspaper.

"There are rumors Dr. Livingstone is dead," Stanley's boss had told him. "Nobody has heard any news from the famous explorer for years. He may be lost in the jungle. If you can find him it'll make sensational headlines!"

Stanley headed straight for Ujiji. "A white man was recently seen here," he was told. **Could it have been Dr. Livingstone?**

When Lake Tanganyika came into Stanley's sight at noon, he and his men marched into Ujiji firing guns to announce their arrival.

Livingstone was lying inside a straw house reading the Bible, his only medicine, when he heard the shots.

Susi rushed in. "Bwana, big caravan

11

is coming down mountain!" he cried.

Livingstone staggered outside into the sunlight. The whole village was in an uproar. Through the trees he caught a glimpse of horses and an endless band of carriers loaded with bales and boxes. This was no merchant caravan!

Moments later, a tall young man in sun helmet and white tropical suit walked straight toward him, stopped, snatched off his helmet and said, **"Dr. Livingstone, I presume?"**

Livingstone smiled and held out his hand. "Welcome to Ujiji!"

"I can't believe it!" exclaimed the young American. "I have walked a thousand miles—and I've found you!"

"Found me?" asked Livingstone puzzled. "Did you think I was lost?"

Dr. Livingstone, so glad to be "found" by Stanley, was thrilled with the abundance of supplies which had been brought to him. "What a miracle," he thought. "God has shown his favor by sending this good Samaritan to me!"

Livingstone enjoyed Stanley's company and his provisions—cookies, jelly, smoked herring and Dutch cheese. Stanley also brought news from the world: The opening of the Suez Canal in 1869, the election of America's new president, General Grant, the laying of the Atlantic telegraph cable between Ireland and Newfoundland.

Stanley asked Livingstone a thousand questions for his article about the explorer. But Livingstone, when warned that Stanley was only interested in making a fortune by selling the story to newspapers around the world, just smiled:

"If so, he's heartily welcome, for it's a great deal more than I could ever make out of myself!"

In the months which followed, the two men explored the northern end of Lake Tanganyika together. Livingstone told Stanley about his earlier travels from **Capetown** in South Africa across the **Kalahari** desert to the Atlantic ocean in the west and the mouth of the **Zambesi** river in the east. He told about his feelings when he first discovered "the smoke that thunders"—the great **Victoria Falls**. He told how terrified he was when a lion once jumped on him, grabbed his left shoulder in its mouth, shook him like a cat shakes a mouse and pinned him to the ground. He told about the hostile **Chiboque** tribe to the southwest who would have killed him and his men with their arrows had he not turned his back to show he was not afraid of them.

One evening, the two men were sitting around the camp fire. The quiet around them was pierced only by the chatter of monkeys in a nearby **mango** tree.

Livingstone's Earlier Travels

The Livingstone family on the edge of the Kalahari

The London Mission Society appointed David Livingstone to help Robert Moffat at Kuruman mission station 700 miles north of Cape Town. As soon as he arrived in 1841, Livingstone began to look north towards "the smoke of a thousand villages," where no missionary had ever been. Two years later, another mission station was built at Mabotsa, 250 miles northeast of Kuruman. The next station was built at Kolobeng, 40 miles north of Mabotsa, where Livingstone made his first and only convert, the Bakwena chief Sechele.

In 1849, Livingstone pushed further north, across the barren Kalahari desert, to discover Lake Ngami. Here the natives told about a "land full of rivers" further north. It was at this point that Livingstone decided his task was to chart the "river highways" of Central Africa rather than build mission stations.

On his next trip north, Livingstone discovered the upper Zambesi, a mighty river 1,000 miles long and 3/4 mile across. Anxious to follow the river east and west, he wondered, Could this be "God's highway" to the hidden peoples in the interior of Africa?

Livingstone's search northwest took him to Luanda on the Atlantic Ocean coast and back straight across Central Africa to Quelimane at the Indian Ocean, a trip that took 20 months and crossed 4,000 miles of unexplored savannah and jungle. Livingstone was the first European to walk across Central Africa—an accomplishment that earned him the National Geographic Society's gold medal and a hero's welcome back in England.

But Livingstone wasn't satisfied. He wanted to prove that the Zambesi was a waterway accessible by steamboat. In 1858 he led an expedition of English scientists up the river to the Kebrabasa Rapids. The rapids stopped the steamer and Livingstone had to give up his Zambesi plan.

Instead he turned to the Nile. When he set out to find the source of the Upper Nile, it was his last chance to track a waterway to the interior of Africa. He died in the attempt.

Four years after Livingstone's death, Henry Stanley traced the White Nile to its source some 8,000 feet up in the mountains above Lake Victoria. By then though, the idea of a riverway to Central Africa had become outdated in favor of land roads and railways.

Livingstone's steamboat "Ma-Robert" on the Zambesi

"Dr. Livingstone, you seem different from other missionaries I've met," said Stanley. "Are you a missionary or an adventurer?"

"Both," answered Livingstone. "Missionaries should always be adventurous." Then he added: "To be honest, I suppose the Mission Society at home thinks I'm not a very successful missionary. After more than 30 years here I have only one convert . . . and not a good one either."

"What do you mean?" asked Stanley.

"**Sechele** was a tribal chief at **Kolobeng**," continued Livingstone. "I stayed with him before crossing the Kalahari desert. He was impressed with my medicine that cured his people, and he listened with interest when I told

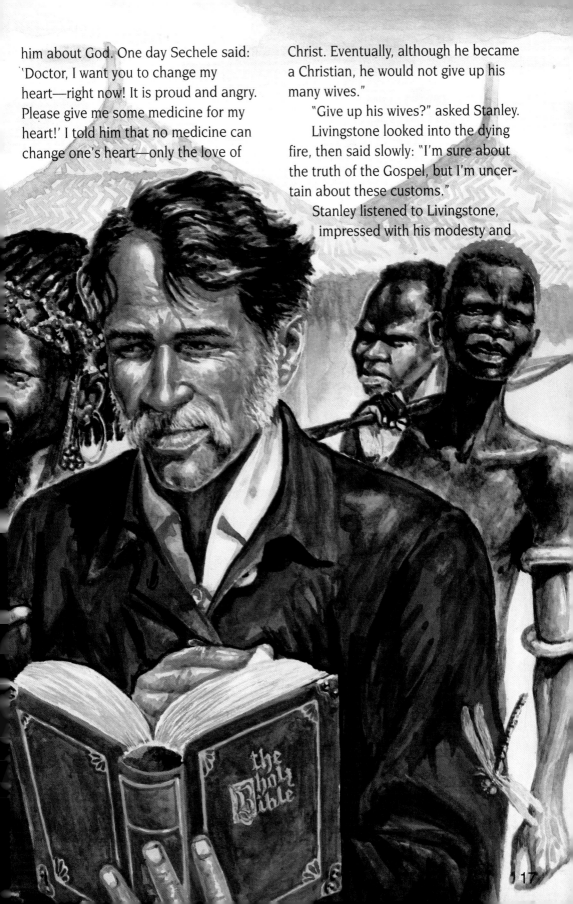

him about God. One day Sechele said: 'Doctor, I want you to change my heart—right now! It is proud and angry. Please give me some medicine for my heart!' I told him that no medicine can change one's heart—only the love of Christ. Eventually, although he became a Christian, he would not give up his many wives."

"Give up his wives?" asked Stanley.

Livingstone looked into the dying fire, then said slowly: "I'm sure about the truth of the Gospel, but I'm uncertain about these customs."

Stanley listened to Livingstone, impressed with his modesty and respect for the African people. Stanley's fascination for the explorer turned into a deep admiration. In his newspaper story published in the New York Herald, Stanley described Livingstone as a hero, almost a saint, in terms of praising his achievements and character.

"For four months and four days," wrote Stanley, "I lived with Livingstone in the same house, same boat, or same tent, and I could find no fault in him."

Stanley's article made headlines around the world. Having "discovered" the discoverer, he became almost as famous.

But Livingstone ignored fame. He felt it was important to direct the world's attention to the cruel slave trade in Africa. And Stanley's article served this cause. Governments in Europe began to recognize the horrors of the slave trade and its long-term consequences for Africa: it was a barrier to peaceful trade and the spreading of the Christian faith.

Livingstone's Family

At a visit in England, 1857. From left to right: Oswell, Livingstone, Thomas, Agnes, Mary and Robert. One child died at birth; another child, Anna Mary, was born the following year.

Almost four years after Livingstone came to Africa he married Robert Moffat's daughter Mary at Kuruman. Mary followed her husband on his travels for seven years and shared his many hardships. During those years they had five children (one died at the age of six weeks).

Mary's health suffered severely, and Livingstone decided to send his family home to England before he set out on his first great journey across Africa. He didn't see them again until he came back to England for a visit four years later.

In 1862 Mary joined her husband on the Zambesi expedition. Four months later she died from malaria and was buried on the bank of the Zambesi. Her death was a terrible blow to Livingstone. Another blow came when Livingstone learned that his oldest son Robert had crossed the Atlantic Ocean and enlisted in the Union Army during the American Civil War—under a false name because he didn't want to "bring further dishonor to the family name." Robert died in a prisoner-of-war camp in South Carolina in 1864.

When Livingstone became older he realized that he had spent too little time with his family. But then it was too late. His children hardly knew him— and they were off on their own.

A STRANGE DISEASE

Africa was on the verge of civil war. Neighboring tribes raided each other's villages to capture people for the traveling slave merchants: mostly Arabs and the Swahili (Africans from the coast). The hunters plunged deeper and deeper into Africa to expand their business, lining up Africans, putting them into iron collars or into "taming sticks" (forked tree branches laid over the slaves' shoulders which closed around their throats with a metal bar). They then drove them to **Zanzibar** from where the slaves were shipped to Arab countries. An estimated 12,000 slaves were exported from Zanzibar every year, despite the British Navy ships in the Indian Ocean trying to stop the slave boats.

Livingstone was helpless against the armed slave traders. The most he could do was aid the abandoned slaves he found along his way. Once he found a woman tied by the neck to a tree, too exhausted to walk on. The Arabs had left her in the scorching sun to die. Another time the doctor saw a three-year-old left behind as the slave hunters dragged her mother away.

Later he found a twelve-year-old boy, left to suffer on the slave trail. Before he died, the boy whispered, "I have pain in my heart."

Dr. Livingstone knew this was a kind of pain he could not cure with any medicine. That night he wrote in his journal: "The strangest disease I have seen in this country is broken-heartedness. This disease attacks free men who have been made slaves . . . it really seems to be broken hearts of which they die."

Livingstone decided that his most important work would be to heal the broken hearts of the Africans. To do this the slave trade had to be stopped. Before persuading the British government to make a greater effort in capturing slave ships, he would have to

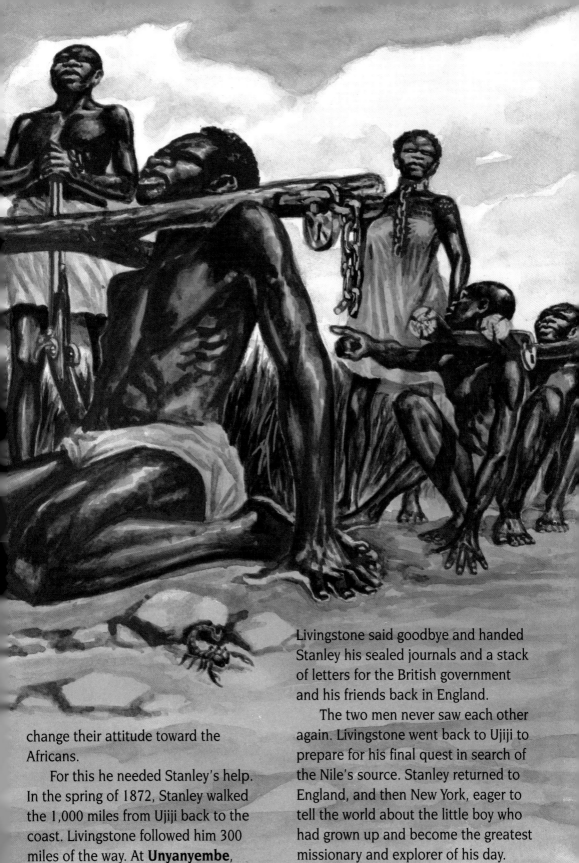

change their attitude toward the Africans.

For this he needed Stanley's help. In the spring of 1872, Stanley walked the 1,000 miles from Ujiji back to the coast. Livingstone followed him 300 miles of the way. At **Unyanyembe**,

Livingstone said goodbye and handed Stanley his sealed journals and a stack of letters for the British government and his friends back in England.

The two men never saw each other again. Livingstone went back to Ujiji to prepare for his final quest in search of the Nile's source. Stanley returned to England, and then New York, eager to tell the world about the little boy who had grown up and become the greatest missionary and explorer of his day.

21

"The Smoke That Thunders"

On his expedition along the Zambesi river toward the Indian Ocean, Livingstone discovered Mosi-oa-tunya or "the smoke that thunders"—the world's greatest waterfall. He renamed it after Victoria, the reigning queen of England.

Victoria Falls is 350 feet deep; 500,000 cubic meters of water pour over the edge of the falls every day. The clouds of mist and vapor rise 300 feet into the air and can be seen ten miles away.

From a little island in the Zambesi, on the very lip of the falls, Livingstone watched this spectacular scenery (which today is counted one of the seven natural wonders of the world) and gave thanks to God. The falls had never before been seen by European eyes. But "scenes so lovely must have been gazed upon by angels in their flight," he wrote.

Livingstone carved his initials and "1855" in a tree on that little island.

NO TIME FOR PLAY

It all began when David Livingstone was born at **Blantyre** near Glasgow, Scotland, on March 19th 1813. When he was ten, he started to work at the Blantyre cotton mill where his father and grandfather had worked. His job was to piece broken threads back together on the spinning machine. His work day began at 6 in the morning and ended at 8 at night. In those days there were no laws against children working, no unions to protect the workers' interests, and no limits on how long a work day could be.

It was terribly hot in the factory and sometimes hard for David and his two brothers to stay awake during their long working hours. David often dreamed about an escape, but he realized the only way was through education. He wanted to be a missionary to a faraway country where no one had been before. He wanted to be a scientist, too. His father had told him about the great need for a whole new kind of missionary: medical preachers who could teach the Word of God as well as heal sickness. David decided to become a missionary doctor.

"Aye lad! Are you dreaming again?"

Caught daydreaming in the factory, David turned around—just in time to get a bucket of cold water in his face.

"Thatta keep ye awaik for a lang time!" grinned the foreman.

As soon as the foreman was out of sight, David pulled out his Latin grammar book and propped it on top of the spinning machine. He took a long look in the book, then walked down the wheels to inspect the thread, his lips moving to repeat what he'd just read.

Every evening at 8, the children who

worked at the Blantyre cotton mill gathered in an adjoining classroom for two hours of school. Most were too tired to learn; but not David. He eagerly prepared for his future by reading every book he could get hold of—especially those about science and nature.

At 10 p.m. David hurried home for five hours of sleep before he would have to be at work again. His family lived in a tiny one-room apartment with a fireplace and two beds, all provided by the mill. This is where David slept alongside his two brothers, two sisters and parents until he was 23 years old.

On Sundays no one worked. After church, David and his brother **Charles** loved to explore the countryside, gathering rocks, plants and insects. One Sunday they came to a quarry where someone was loading rocks into a wheelbarrel.

"Look, Charles!" said David as he picked up a rock. "There are seashells in this stone."

"Seashells?" wondered Charles.

"Why are there seashells here when the ocean is fifty miles away?"

The man loading the rocks answered, "When the good Lord made the rocks, he made those shells and put them there!"

David laughed and said, "Aye Charles, there's science for you!"

Charles turned around. "Why are you laughing, Davy? Those science

books have turned your head. See what that has done to your religion! Don't you still believe that God created the world?"

"Oh yes," answered David and put the rock into his pocket, "but the quarryman skipped the real explanation. The shells in the rock prove that a long time ago, the sea covered this area. When it receded, the sand grew hard— and the shells were trapped inside the rock. To accept that, Charles, is not to deny God created the world. It only confirms there is logic and order in all his creation!"

By the time David turned 23 he had saved enough money to quit the mill and go to school in the city. His father walked him to Glasgow eight miles away and helped him find a tiny room in a poor area called Rotten Row.

27

MISSIONARY AT LAST

Four years later, Livingstone passed his final medical exams. The **London Missionary Society** appointed a minister who would teach him to preach. One evening when he entered the pulpit at Stanford Rivers, Livingstone forgot his memorized sermon. "Friends . . . I have forgotten all I had to say!" he stammered and rushed out.

But shortly before his missionary training was completed, Livingstone listened to the preaching of a successful missionary on leave from South Africa, **Robert Moffat**. After the meeting, Livingstone told Moffat he was soon to be a medical missionary, but did not know where to go.

"Mr. Moffat," he asked politely, "do you think I would do for Africa?"

Moffat's answer shaped the vision that would guide Livingstone for the next 33 years: "Yes," said Moffat, "if you don't settle, but advance to unknown territory. In the morning sun, on the vast plain to the north of my station, I have seen the smoke of a thousand villages where no missionary has ever been!"

In November 1840, Livingstone was licensed as a physician—although he nearly failed because of an argument with his professors about how to use the stethoscope. The next morning he boarded a steamer for London, then the sailing ship George, heading for Cape Town, South Africa.

PRESSING ON

Thirty-two years later—at Unyanyembe where Stanley had left him that last time—Livingstone sensed he'd come close to the end of his journey. While waiting the five months for new carriers, he read and observed everything around him: the African children's games, the tribal customs, and the geological structure of the land.

The doctor's plan was simple. As soon as the carriers showed up he would press southwest around the southern tip of Lake Tanganyika and onto the copper mines of **Katanga**. "Only eight days' journey from there are the great springs you're looking for," the natives told him. He would follow the Lualaba river north, hoping to find it emptied into the Nile. Then he would retire and return to England.

The Mysterious Nile

The Nile river is the longest river in the world (2,160 miles). Along its lower course rose one of the earliest civilizations some 8,000 years ago. But the river's upper course remained unknown to Europeans for thousands of years.

Since the days of the Egyptian pharaohs, explorers and geographers had speculated about the location of the Nile's source. No one knew for sure. The Greek historian Herodotus, in the 5th century BC, told about two mysterious hills in Africa's interior with sharp conical tops. Between them, he believed, lay the fountains of the Nile. The Egyptian geographer Ptolemy, in the 2nd century AD, claimed that the Nile rose from two great lakes at the foot of the "Mountains of the Moon" south of the equator. These ancient theories

Yet Livingstone never returned. For a long time he had been continually sick and he suffered from internal bleeding. "I'm ill with bowels," he wrote, "having eaten nothing for eight days." The journal entries became shorter each day. The rainy season set in. His men had to carry him through floods and swamps thick with papyrus and lotus plants while searching for dry ground.

One night the caravan made camp beside a hill of fierce safari ants, known for their painful bite. Livingstone wanted to prove that the ants would not bite unless they were provoked. He let the ants swarm over his foot. Soon his whole body was covered. It took his men two hours to get the biting ants off of him.

All winter Livingstone pressed on, advancing only a mile a day. Determined to reach his goal, though, he wrote, "I encourage myself in the

went unchallenged until the 18th century.

In 1770, the Scottish explorer James Bruce traced the origin of the river's northern branch (the Blue Nile) to the highlands of Ethiopia. Still a much longer branch (the White Nile) was believed to rise far to the south.

In 1858 the British explorer John Speke discovered Lake Victoria which he believed was the source of the White Nile. Eight years later, when Livingstone set out on his last journey, he was determined to prove that Speke was wrong. Livingstone believed that the Nile rose further southwest, by

the copper mines of Katanga. He died on his way there.

After Livingstone's death, his friend Henry Stanley continued the search around Lake Tanganyika and Lake Victoria. Stanley once and for all settled the ancient mystery. John Speke had been right: Lake Victoria was the fountainhead of the White Nile.

Stanley circumsailing Lake Victoria

Lord my God, and go forward."

By April, no longer able to go forward, Livingstone had his men make a stretcher and carry him as he groaned from the pain. When they reached the village of Chief **Chitambo**, they knew it was no use carrying their leader any further. **Chuma** and Susi, the two faithful men who had been with him so long, built a large hut and brought him his most precious possessions: his Bible, geographical instruments, rifle, medicine chest and metal-backed notebook. Finally on Sunday, April 27th 1873, David Livingstone wrote his last entry: "Knocked up quite . . . . We are

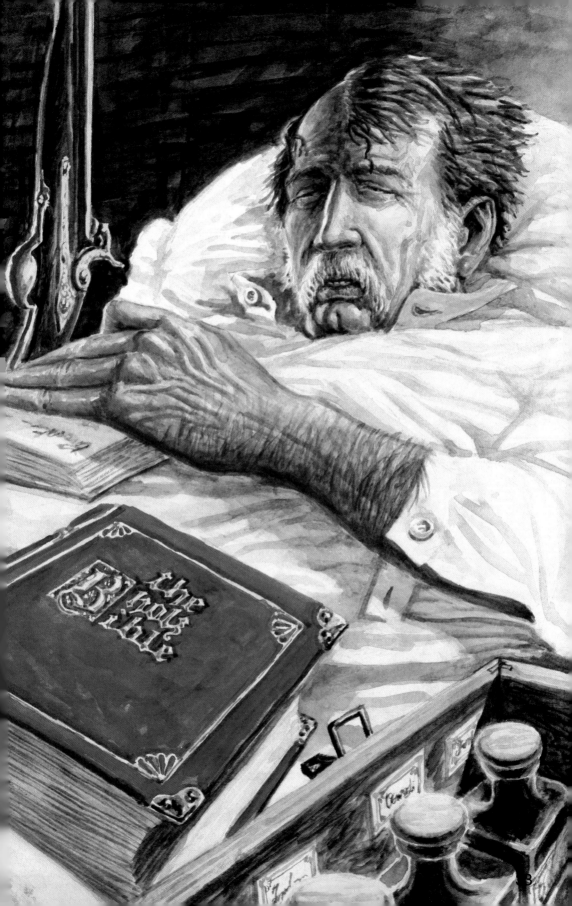

on the banks of River Molilamo."

Three days later, Livingstone was drifting deliriously in and out of sleep. At 11 p.m., noise woke the doctor and he called for Susi.

"Are our men making that noise?" he asked faintly.

"No," said Susi, "the villagers are scaring a buffalo away from their fields."

The doctor was drifting. "Is this the Luapula river?" he asked.

"No, not yet," replied Susi.

Then the doctor asked in Swahili:

"**Siku ngapi kuenda Luapula?**" (How many days to the Luapula?)

"**Na zani ziku tatu, Bwana!**" (I think three days, master!)

"Oh dear, dear," sighed the doctor in great pain.

The next morning before dawn, on May 1st 1873, Susi found the doctor kneeling by the side of his bed, body stretched forward and head buried in his hands. Susi went forward and gently put his hand on the doctor's cheek. It was almost cold.

Dr. David Livingstone was dead.

THE FINAL JOURNEY HOME

Chuma and Susi carried their dead leader outside. The local villagers of Chitambo mourned the doctor's death, waving bows and spears. For two hours drumming and wailing filled the air. Then **Farjala**, the doctor's assistant who had observed once how he opened up a body to determine the cause of death, cut Livingstone's chest, drew out the heart and intestines and buried them in a tin box under an African mvula tree.

Jacob, a former slave freed by Livingstone and trained by missionaries, read the burial service from the doctor's prayer book—determined to show the respect he would show any great African chief. Then the Africans rubbed the body with salt and anointed it with brandy from the medicine chest in order to prepare it for travel back to Livingstone's own people.

For two weeks the body was left to dry in the sun, then it was covered with an animal skin and fitted into a cylinder of bark from a myonga tree. Finally it

was wrapped in sailcloth, painted with tar and lashed on poles. The party set out for the coast at Zanzibar 1,550 miles away. Nine months later they arrived and were welcomed by 700 freed slaves who had come down to say goodbye to the missionary who showed them the love of the Christian God.

Eleven months after his death, the remains of the famous explorer finally arrived in England to receive a hero's funeral in Westminster Abbey. He was mourned by the entire country.

But Livingstone's faithful servants back in Africa also mourned. His heart was buried in African soil, at the roots of a fine mvula tree.

SUCCESS AT LAST

That dark morning at Chitambo, when Livingstone buried his head in his hands and died, he must have believed he had failed. Not only were the geographical questions he had struggled with still unanswered; the mission work he had come to establish had failed, and the Arab slave trade had not been stopped.

Livingstone's journals

If only he could have known that within five years of his death all three problems would be solved—all due to his persistent pioneering work! The Lualaba river was traced to the **River Congo** by his friend **Verney Cameron**. The source of the Nile was confirmed to be Lake Victoria by his friend Stanley. New mission societies were started and stations popped up all over Central Africa. And in 1876 the slave market at Zanzibar was effectively shut down, partly due to another friend, **John Kirk**.

Livingstone's journals and letters provide detailed knowledge of the plants, rocks, insects and animals of Africa—as well as its people and their tribal customs. The vast blank areas which had until then been marked "Unexplored" was filled in by Livingstone with highlands, valleys, lakes, mountains, forests and hundreds of rivers.

Africa after Livingstone

Livingstone never showed interest in the political development of the land he was exploring; he never hoisted a flag or claimed any land in the name of the British government. Livingstone assumed Africa belonged to the Africans. Yet the "scramble for Africa" was a tragic result of his pioneering work.

After Livingstone's death, his friend Henry Morton Stanley was hired by King Leopold II of

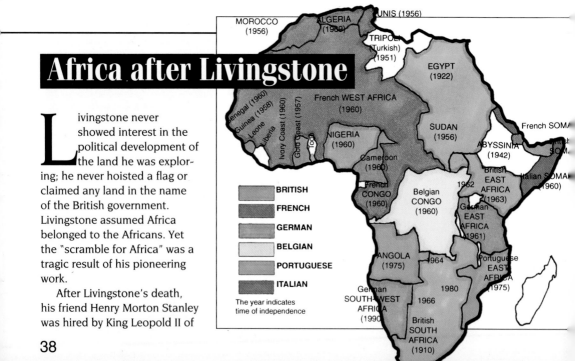

MOROCCO (1956)
ALGERIA (1980)
TUNIS (1956)
TRIPOLI (Turkish) (1951)
EGYPT (1922)
French WEST AFRICA (1960)
Senegal (1960)
Guinea (1958)
Sierra Leone
Liberia
Ivory Coast (1960)
Gold Coast (1957)
Togo
NIGERIA (1960)
SUDAN (1956)
ABYSSINIA (1942)
French SOMA.
British SOM.
Italian SOMA. (1960)
Cameroon (1960)
French CONGO (1960)
Belgian CONGO (1960)
British EAST AFRICA 1962 (1963)
German EAST AFRICA (1961)
ANGOLA (1975)
1964
Portuguese EAST AFRICA (1975)
German SOUTH-WEST AFRICA (1990)
1966
1980
British SOUTH AFRICA (1910)

BRITISH
FRENCH
GERMAN
BELGIAN
PORTUGUESE
ITALIAN

The year indicates time of independence

What set Livingstone apart from other explorers of his time was not just his many impressive discoveries, but a rare sympathy and understanding towards the African people whose languages and customs he had learned. When Livingstone died, a new attitude in white Europe was born—respect for the African people and a growing willingness to treat them as equals.

Livingstone paid a high price for his dream of setting Africa free. He gave up a career among his own people and exchanged comfort and conveniences for hardships and sickness, even to the point of feeling abandoned by God. Yet Livingstone accomplished more through his apparent failure than most men accomplish with their success.

"Westminster Abbey had opened her doors to men who have played larger and greater parts in the history of mankind," wrote a London newspaper on the day of his funeral, "but the feeling amongst many this afternoon was, that seldom has been admitted one more worthy—one more unselfish in his devotion to duty—one whose ruling desire was to benefit his kind and advance the sum of knowledge and civilization—than the brave, modest, self-sacrificing, African explorer."

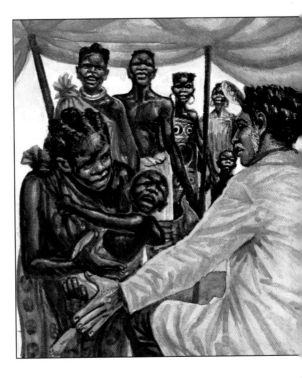

Belgium to explore "the Congo region's possibilities for development." In reality, the king was looking for a colony—and since Stanley was looking for an investor for his next expedition, he accepted the royal match.

While Stanley marched through the vast Congo Basin between Lake Tanganyika and the Atlantic coast, King Leopold founded the "International African Association" of scientists and geographers. In practice, it was a disguise for the king's personal economical and political interests in Africa. Leopold succeeded in securing the Congo Basin for himself.

In 1885, at a Berlin meeting between fourteen European powers, Africa was carved into European colonies: France took the northwestern part; Belgium a slice of the western part; Britain and Germany part of the east. After World War I, the German territories were given up to the others.

The "scramble" was a smash-and-grab enterprise with no rules except diplomatic rhetoric—and with no regard for the wishes of African chiefs who had been ruling the land for centuries.

Along with colonization came civilization and its promised blessings of economic development, hygiene, trade, railways, missionaries, education, and the abolition of the slave trade. Within a few years Africa was being pulled from the stone age into the industrial age—and it's hard to say whether Africa's own peoples gained or lost in the process. Today, as the African countries are becoming independent from their European colonizers, they are struggling for identity and democracy.

*"I go back to Africa to try to open a path
for commerce and Christianity; do you
carry out the work which I have begun!
I leave it with you!"*

(Livingstone, Cambridge University address, 1857)

41

Main Events in Livingstone's Life

1813 David Livingstone is born on March 19 at Blantyre, Scotland.

1823 Livingstone starts working in Blantyre Cotton Mill.

1836 Livingstone enlists at the university in Glasgow.

1840 After his medical exam and missionary training Livingstone sails for South Africa.

1841 Livingstone arrives at Kuruman mission station. Henry Stanley is born in Wales.

1843 Livingstone builds frontier station at Mabotsa.

1845 Livingstone marries Mary Moffat.

1849 Livingstone crosses the Kalahari desert.

1851 Livingstone discovers the upper Zambesi and Victoria Falls.

1853-56 Livingstone crosses Africa between Luanda (Angola) and Quelimane (Mozambique).

1856-58 Livingstone visits England and is received as a hero.

1858-63 The Zambesi expedition fails.

1862 Mary Livingstone dies at the Zambesi.

1864 Livingstone visits England for the last time. His son Robert dies in the American Civil War.

1865 Livingstone goes back to Africa to find the source of the Nile river.

1871 Livingstone is "found" by Stanley.

1873 Livingstone dies at Chitambo on May 1.

1874 Livingstone is buried in Westminster Abbey, London.

BOOK RESOURCES

David Livingstone, Missionary Travels and Researches in South Africa (1857)
David and Charles Livingstone, Narrative of an Expedition to the Zambesi and its Tributaries (1865)
David Livingstone, The Last Journals of David Livingstone in Central Africa (1874)
Jack Simmons, Livingstone and Africa (1955)
Jeanette Eaton, David Livingstone (1947)
Richard Humble, The Travels of Livingstone (1991)
East Africa (Time/Life 1987)
Susan Clinton, The World's Great Explorers: Henry Stanley and David Livingstone (1990)
Thomas Pakenham, The Scramble for Africa (1991)

R. Nile

Lake Albert

Mt. Kilimanjaro

R. Lualaba

R. Congo

Lake Edward

Lake Victoria

Nyangwe

Ujiji
Unyanyembe

Zanzibar

Lake Tanganyika
Lake Mweru

Lake Nyasa

R. Luapula

Chitambo

R. Zambesi

Kebrabasa rapids

R. Shire

MARY LIVINGSTONE

Sesheke

Victoria falls

D.L. 1855

Quilimane

Kalahari Desert

INDIAN OCEAN

Lake Ngami

Kolobeng

LIVINGSTONE'S AFRICA

Mabotsa

Miles

Kuruman

R. Orange

100   200   300   400   500